THE MAGDALENE SERMON

THE MAGDALENE SERMON AND EARLIER POEMS

Eiléan Ní Chuilleanáin

WAKE FOREST UNIVERSITY PRESS

WAKE FOREST UNIVERSITY PRESS
WINSTON-SALEM, N. C. 27109

This book, published in association with
Gallery Press, is for sale only in the United States of America.

Part One *The Magdalene Sermon* first published by The
Gallery Press in Ireland in 1989. The Poems in Part Two,
some revised, from *The Rose Geranium* first published by
The Gallery Press in Ireland in 1981.

ISBN 0-916390-44-6 (cloth)
ISBN 0-916390-43-8 (paper)
LC Card Number 90-072090

Cover and title page design by Richard Murdoch.
Text designed by Peter Fallon and typeset by
Redsetter Ltd. of Ireland.

Contents

PART ONE *The Magdalene Sermon*

Pygmalion's Image   *page* 9
The Liturgy 10
History 11
Observations from Galileo 12
Crossing 13
The Pig-boy 14
Permafrost Woman 15
Street 16
The Hill-town 17
Snow 18
MacMoransbridge 19
Looking at the Fall 20
Balloon 21
London 22
River, with Boats 23
The Italian Kitchen 24
Recovery 25
Quarant' Ore 26
A Voice 27
In Rome 28
J'ai Mal à nos Dents 29
Consolation 30
Fallen Tree in a Churchyard 32
St Mary Magdalene Preaching at Marseilles 33
So She Looked, in that Company 34
Chrissie 35
The Informant 36
A Whole Life 38
Those People 39
The Promise 40

PART TWO *The Rose-Geranium*

The Last Glimpse of Erin 45
'He Hangs in Shades the Orange Bright' 46
March 18th 1977 47
1. Like One Borne Away in a Dance and Veiled 48
2. She Opened the Egg 49
3. Willaupuis 50
4. The Rose-Geranium 51
5. The Pebble Skips 52
6. Circus 53
7. Waters Between 54
8. Waking 55
9. Overmantel 56
10. Skeleton Walk 57
11. Talking to the Skin 58
12. War's Annals Fading 59
13. Feeding the Cats 60
14. Amelia 61
15. The Bare Deal Board 62

PART ONE

The Magdalene Sermon

in loving memory of
Katherine Kavanagh
1928-1989

Pygmalion's Image

Not only her stone face, laid back staring in the ferns,
But everything the scoop of the valley contains begins to move
(And beyond the horizon the trucks beat the highway.)

A tree inflates gently on the curve of the hill;
An insect crashes on the carved eyelid;
Grass blows westward from the roots,
As the wind knifes under her skin and ruffles it like a book.

The crisp hair is real, wriggling like snakes;
A rustle of veins, tick of blood in the throat;
The lines of the face tangle and catch, and
A green leaf of language comes twisting out of her mouth.

The Liturgy

He has been invited to perform
The very ancient ceremony, the Farewell to Fire,
And with misgivings has agreed.

The day comes and doubt comes back.
He never thought his initiation
Would lead to this, he planned a quiet life
Studying the epigrams incised
On millennial plaques. And that
Is the reason he was asked to officiate;
The devotees in their casual search
Had spotted the sacred metal in his luggage.

He stands in the September afternoon glow, balancing
The copper shells and their ritual pouch in two hands,
Then clatters off down the stairs of the hostel.

They are waiting outside, the muffled band,
Their boat moored and loaded
With piled blankets, crocheted shawls,
Nets of mellowed fruit. Behind them,
The glitter of the estuary, the honeycomb
Of cliffs riddled with sunlight.

Meanwhile the house is empty
Except for the two women on the ground floor.
The latch of their room will never shut completely.
They hear the hinges of the big door closing,
They know the length of the ceremony, they know
They have just forty minutes.

History

Accept the gift
Ancestral flood
Parting the ground
Washing the living
Shearing the bank of ghosts —

These will not cauterise a wound.

The fire polluted you
With menstrual stain
Dirt from forges
Ashes fat and bones
From the invaders' feast.

The leaves of yellow metal
Were floated to us on the stream
Our grandmothers wrote in them
With reeds and vinegar —
That is a lost art

Our history is a mountain of salt
A leaking stain under the evening cliff
It will be gone in time
Grass will grow there —

Not in our time.

Observations from Galileo

1

If two such bodies are to touch each other
They will touch at one point only. This is plain
Though we do not know what they are, or if one
Looking like a dry fist of asphalt
Is in fact our tidal earth. Even so,
Over all her wild complexion there is only
One point where a man is proving, with basins of water
And sun reflected on a whitewashed wall,
As the servants draw long curtains back,
That such great bodies have their currents,
They feel corruption though they spell our time.

2

But who has not seen, in a city at night,
Returning home, how the moon jumps
From a gable to a high wall, keeps pace as you go,
Running along the rim of the wall like a cat?

Crossing

He thought his death near then, his life seemed
Like a drop within him, nearly at the dregs,
The stopper lost and the air sucking it dry.

I walked in the plantation with him and his grown children
To a graceful house burnt-out, Currah Chase,
Blunt on its eminence among the young spruce.

When we came to the neat locked gate
He climbed it without pausing, and we followed
His tracks to the ruin, its black windows lying

Open as the ornamental water below
To the *droit de seigneur* of the visiting swans —
The breeze rising, airing the cellars.

The Pig-boy

It was his bag of tricks she wanted, surely not him:
The pipkin that sat on the flame, its emissions
Transporting her so she skipped from kitchen to kitchen
Sampling licks of food; she knew who had bacon
And who had porridge and tea. And she needed
The swoop of light from his torch
That wavered as she walked,
Booted, through the evening fair,
Catching the green flash of sheeps' eyes,
The glow of false teeth in the skull:

Its grotto light stroked oxters of arches,
Bridges, lintels, probed cobbles of tunnels
Where the world shook itself inside out like a knitted sleeve:
Light on the frozen mesh, the fishbone curve, the threads
And weights.
           And as day
Glittered on the skin, she stood
In the hood of a nostril and saw
The ocean gleam of his eye.

Permafrost Woman

Now, that face he coursed
Beyond all the lapping
Voices, through linear deserts

Unfolds among peaks
Of frozen sea, the wave
Coiling upward its wrinkled grace.

Dumb cliffs tell their story, split and reveal
Fathomed straits. The body opens its locks.

Spying the crowded
Ocean graveyard, wrecks shifting
A sea mile to the west as the blow falls,

The traveller feels
His hair bend at the fresh weight
Of snow, the wind is an intimate fist

Brushing back strands: he stares at the wide mouth, packed
With grinding ash: the landslide of his first dream.

Street

He fell in love with the butcher's daughter
When he saw her passing by in her white trousers
Dangling a knife on a ring at her belt.
He stared at the dark shining drops on the paving-stones.

One day he followed her
Down the slanting lane at the back of the shambles.
A door stood half-open
And the stairs were brushed and clean,
Her shoes paired on the bottom step,
Each tread marked with the red crescent
Her bare heels left, fading to faintest at the top.

The Hill-town

The bus floats away on the big road and leaves her
In sunlight, the only moving thing to be seen.

The girl at her kitchen-window in the ramparts
Can glimpse her through a steep rift between houses.
She turns to salt the boiling water
As her mother begins to climb, dark blue in the blue shade,
Past the shut doors and the open windows,
Their sounds of knife and glass.
She crosses into the sun before passing
The blank shutters of the glazier's house.

He is in there, has heard her step and
Paused, with the sharp tool in his hand.
He stands, his fingers pressed against the looking-glass
Like a man trying to hold up a falling building
That is not even a reflection now.

Their child knows where to glance, turning off the flame,
To spot her mother, a wrinkle in the light.
She remembers lying in the wide bed, three years old,
The sound of water and the gas going silent,
And the morning was in the white sieve of the curtain
Where a shadow moved, her mother's body, wet patches
Blotting the stretched cloth, shining like dawn.

Snow

'I thought of you then,' she says, 'flocking
On the edge of the same water —
The yearly walk by the banks — '
As she stood by the calm water
And the snow kept faltering past,
And past the window where a man's bare arm
Reached for clothes and for matches.

'I heard him calling,' she says; 'I stood there, planted,
Marking time.' She spotted, between the branches,
How the treecreeper survives by its own rites.
The beak tapped, the wedge of time sank.

She thought of them, crowding the cold shore
With pilgrimage, like migrant birds,
Their habitat a shrinking blot on the map,
The tidal ogham in their feathers
A message for the watcher, keeping score.

MacMoransbridge

Although the whole house creaks from their footsteps
The sisters, when he died,
Never hung up his dropped dressing-gown,
Took the ash from the grate, or opened his desk. His will,
Clearly marked, and left in the top drawer,
Is a litany of objects lost like itself.
The tarnished silver teapot, to be sold
And the money given to a niece for her music-lessons,
Is polished and used on Sundays. The rings and pendants
Devised by name to each dear sister are still
Tucked between silk scarves in his wardrobe, where he found
And hid them again, the day they buried his grandmother.
And his posthumous plan of slights and surprises
Has failed – though his bank account's frozen – to dam up time.

He had wanted it all to stop,
As he stopped moving between that room
With its diaries and letters posted abroad
And the cold office over the chemist's
Where he went to register deaths and births,

While the sisters went on as they do now, never
All resting at once – one of them would be
Boiling up mutton-shanks for broth, or washing out blankets,
Dipping her black clothes in boiled vitriol and oak-gall
(He used to see from his leafy window
Shoulders bobbing at the pump like pistons).
And still the youngest goes down at night to the stream,
Tending the salmon-nets at the weir,
And comes home to bed as the oldest of all
Can already be heard adding up small change with the servant.

Looking at the Fall

She stood again in the briar path,
Her child in her hand, and looked over
Where the water struck the rock, where
The divided leaf struck root, and saw
The shielded home of the spider surviving
Below the curve of the fall. She said,
What will it be when summer turns
The scapula to a dry bone?

Look, don't touch, she said to the reaching child.
Across her eye a shadow fell like a door closing upstream,
A lock slipping, a high stack of water
Loosed, spinning down, to slam them out of breath.

She looked again at the fall –
The rock half dry, the skein of water
Crooked and white – and saw
The ribs of a candle,
The flame blown adrift,
A draught from a warped door.

She looked at the rock and saw bone
And saw the bones piled in the mountainside
And the cross wind cutting at the roots,
Whistling in the dry bed of the stream.

Balloon

Let the child sleep now
The judge has finished, the papers are signed,
The cameras done flashing
On him as he held on tightly
To his lighter-than-air balloon.

Warm currents of his room
Shake the flagging lost balloon, revive
A floated search, coasting
From shelf, past open door, to rest
On a dance-floor, held and freed

By a loose jet of air.
Twisting the whiskered angles of toys,
Of musical instruments resting,
The silk lobe flutters not quite down to earth:
A big strange fish gleams, filling the child's bed.

London

At fifty, she misses the breast
That grew in her thirteenth year
And was removed last month. She misses
The small car she drove through the seaside town
And along cliffs for miles. In London
She will not take the tube, is afraid of taxis.

We choose a random bar. She sits by me,
Looking along the jacketed line of men's
Lunchtime backs, drinks her vermouth.
I see her eye slide to the left;
At the counter's end sits a high metal urn.

What are you staring at? That polished curve,
The glint wavering on steel, the features
Of our stranger neighbour distorted.
You can't see it from where you are.
When that streak of crooked light
Goes out, my life is over.

1981

River, with Boats

Of course she does not mind sleeping
On the deep fur of the bed
Beside the wide window
Where the birds hop,
Where the boats pass.

She can hear the hooters
Down there in a greeting;
She can see a flash of the river,
A glitter on the ceiling
When the wind blows
And the high branches of trees
On the other bank
Skip and bow in circles.

Only at the highest tide
The window is blocked
By the one framed eye
Of a tethered coaster
Swaying and tugging and flapping with the wind,
And the faces of the mariners
Crowd at the glass like fishes.

The Italian Kitchen

Time goes by the book laid open
On the long marble table: my work
In the kitchen your landlord painted yellow and white.
Beyond it the glass cupboard doors: behind them now
Ranged the green and yellow cups and plates
You bought in September and left behind, still in boxes.

One more of your suddenly furnished houses.
Eighteen years since we discovered, cash in hand,
Anonymous, the supermarket pleasures
Stacked and shinily wrapped, right
For this country, where all wipes clean,
Dries fast. Or California where you are now.

No sound from the man asleep upstairs.
At the hour's end I walk to the window
Looking over the slopes. Now the night mist
Rises off the vague plain, reaching
Our tall pine where cones cling like mussels:

Light still plays among the branches,
Touches the cold cheek of the window-pane.
I've bought blankets and firewood; we live here now.

Agello, March 1981

Recovery

A month since the hospital sleep
When I looked down on pain,
When dreams were riddled,
The pain could be a dream:
We sit so far away at a balcony table,
A succession of light dishes evolves
From salt to sweet, tasting of,
Trailing into the future, and we turn
To look down. The many-coloured women
Rinse and spread their light garments,
The river limps off between sandbanks
Yet turns a small millwheel.

A flight of steps shrugs down to the water-level,
Each one a pause, a window on the air,
The sun tangling cogs of light, the water
Angling at a small cloud
Never again to be so clearly seen.

Quarant' Ore

At the dark early hour
When the open door of the church
Is pumping out light,
The sacristan is at work unfolding
The stacked chairs, he carries them
Out of the porch, into the glow.
They spread wide like daisies,
They turn to the wide gold rose.
Follow it, ranked in rings.

And still it is not day
And the morning papers are lying
Dropped by gates in grey piles,
When the first pilgrims arrive,
Slipping into the dark shell of the porch,
To squat on the stone –
The practised knees doubled against the breastbone,
The elbows not interfering. They are packed
Lightly as drifted rubbish in corners.
They never obscure the blazing outline
Of the arch lying open for the real congregation
To roll up punctually in cars,
The knights with medals and white gloves.

A Voice

1
Having come this far, in response
To a woman's voice, a distant wailing,
Now he thinks he can distinguish words:
   You may come in –
   You are already in.

But the wall is thornbushes, crammed, barbed.
A human skeleton, warped in a dive, is clasped
In the grip of a flowery briar. His wincing flesh
Reproves him, turns and flows
Backwards like a tide.

2
Knowing it now for a trick of the light
He marches forward, takes account of
True stones and mortared walls,
Downfaces the shimmer
And shakes to hear the voice humming again:

In the bed of the stream
She lies in her bones –
Wide bearing hips and square
Elbows. Around them lodged,
Gravegoods of horsehair and an ebony peg.

'What sort of ornament is this?
What sort of mutilation? Where's
The muscle that called up the sound,
The tug of hair and the turned cheek?'
The sign persists, in the ridged fingerbone.

And he hears her voice, a wail of strings.

In Rome

The Pope's musketeers are breaking their fast
On the roof above my bed. Harsh burning of kebabs
Reeks down through the gap in the beams, and the retching
Of their caged doves. The captain lowered some charcoal
Last night; my poor girls are cooking eggs now
Behind the screen. Soon they must wrap
And veil up for the street, for the hours lounging
Nibbling bread in the Cardinal's front hall,
Twisting to keep their heels out of sight.

Then I have time to walk, alone on the carpet
On half the floor, where we eat and sleep together.
Not even the mice scramble on the clean boards.
We keep the bell-shrine there, and the gold chasubles
For the feast day. I must not go out.
But from the egg-shaped window
I can see the girls trailing back home, with a promise.

Indeed, only an hour after the markets close
The deaf runner from the palace climbs
With two silver pieces and odd coppers.
When we were at home it would have been three sheep –
Work for the troop, skinning, washing the guts,
Digging the pit for the fire. When the meat was eaten,
The wool to card and spin.
I am obliged to God for inventing the city,
To the Cardinal for the sound of money,
The clipped rounds, the battered profiles:
They circle my sleep like the faces of lost kin.

J'ai Mal à nos Dents

in memory of Anna Cullinane (Sister Mary Antony)

The Holy Father gave her leave
To return to her father's house
At seventy-eight years of age.

When young in the Franciscan house at Calais
She complained to the dentist, *I have a pain in our teeth*
– Her body dissolving out of her first mother,
Her five sisters aching at home.

Her brother listened to news
Five times in a morning on Radio Éireann
In Cork, as the Germans entered Calais.
Her name lay under the surface, he could not see her
Working all day with the sisters,
Stripping the hospital, loading the sick on lorries,
While Reverend Mother walked the wards and nourished them
With jugs of wine to hold their strength.
J'étais à moitié saoûle. It was done,
They lifted the old sisters on to the pig-cart
And the young walked out on the road to Desvres,
The wine still buzzing and the planes over their heads.

Je mangerai les pissenlits par les racines.
A year before she died she lost her French accent
Going home in her habit to care for her sister Nora
(Une malade à soigner une malade).
They handed her back her body,
Its voices and its death.

Consolation

His wife collects the rifled
Remains. The list accounted for,
His pockets emptied, their load (codes,
Lists, cards, his multiplied signature)
Locked up for her claiming,
It seems little was taken.
Between the pages of his passport
A copy of his deposition
Typed on the day of the incident, on a loud machine
By an irritated sergeant.

She asks the nun, 'But was that what killed him,
A blow on the head?' Alive,
Three days ago he asked the sergeant,
'What about the blow from behind?'
'No sir, the boy just landed from above you
    and snatched your wallet.'
'I felt it as a blow.'

He was still in the weavers' alley,
Turning to look past hanging cloth down an entry –
A burrow, green light at the end,
A sliver of an arch
Crossed by one trickling thread,
A segment of shoulder and arm –
And his shoulder felt the force, like a wall falling.

The hospital basement is vaulted and pillared:
A wide crypt, old and clean. The nun sits down
To rifle a desk for the right form of receipt.
'It was just as if he waited for the priest to come.'
'He was quite collected, he spoke sensibly.'

She hears the words, the repeated story:
There was no assassination, the fire in his brain
Came only from the red of the dyed cloth.
There was a pillared space when he was dying,
A voice and a response. It was not a hunt and a blow.

Fallen Tree in a Churchyard

in memoriam John Jordan

The tree falls, and
The daylight searches
Where once the roots
Discreetly moved one way
As a blind man's hand
Through a cat's coat.

The tangle, the drying clay
Coating the major passages
Never until now shaped
By flood or storm,
Becomes finally
Visible, halved
By the acute
Maker of threads, tier of knots,
Binder of air and earth:

We can see it now,
Forked and completed.

St Mary Magdalene Preaching at Marseilles

Now at the end of her life she is all hair –
A cataract flowing and freezing – and a voice
Breaking loose from the loose red hair,
The secret shroud of her skin:
A voice glittering in the wilderness.
She preaches in the city, she wanders
Late in the evening through shaded squares.

The hairs on the back of her wrists begin to lie down
And she breathes evenly, her elbows leaning
On a smooth wall. Down there in the piazza,
The boys are skimming on toy carts, warped
On their stomachs, like breathless fish.

She tucks her hair around her,
Looking beyond the game
To the suburban marshes.

Out there a shining traps the sun,
The waters are still clear,
Not a hook or a comma of ice
Holding them, the water-weeds
Lying collapsed like hair
At the turn of the tide;

They wait for the right time, then
Flip all together their thousands of sepia feet.

So She Looked, in that Company

Seeing her here
I know at once who she must be.
She does not move while
The pale figures out of the anthologies
In their coarse shirts are paraded
To tell their hesitant stories
Twisting the grammar of their exotic speech.

They line up as if
Back to the wall were the only possible stance.
Their throats are scarred and their voices
Birdlike.
        – Until the viewing is over,
The woman waits to be taken away,
Then they can be heard, heartily chatting
Among themselves, calling for big jugs of drink.

Chrissie

Escaped beyond hope, she climbs now
Back over the ribs of the wrecked ship,
Kneels on the crushed afterdeck, between gross
Maternal coils: the scaffolding
Surviving after pillage.
                        On the strand
The voices buzz and sink; heads can be seen
Ducking into hutches, bent over boiling pans.
The trees above the sand, like guests,
Range themselves, flounced, attentive.
Four notches down the sky, the sun gores the planks;
Light fills the growing cavity
That swells her, that ripens to her ending.

The tide returning shocks the keel;
The timbers gape again, meeting the salty breeze;
She lies where the wind rips at her left ear,
Her skirt flapping, the anchor-fluke
Biting her spine; she hears
The dull sounds from the island change
To a shrill evening cry. In her head she can see them
Pushing out boats, Mother Superior's shoulder to the stern
(Her tanned forehead more dreadful now
Than when helmeted and veiled)
                        And she goes on fingering
In the shallow split in the wood
The grandmother's charm, a stone once shaped like a walnut,
They had never found. Salt water soaked its force:
The beat of the oars cancelled its landward grace.

She clings, as once to the horned altar beside the well.

The Informant

Underneath the photograph
Of the old woman at her kitchen table
With a window beyond (fuchsias, a henhouse, the sea)
Are entered: her name and age, her late husband's occupation
(A gauger), her birthplace, not here
But in another parish, near the main road.
She is sitting with tea at her elbow
And her own fairy-cakes, baked that morning
For the young man who listens now to the tape
Of her voice changing, telling the story,
And hears himself asking,
Did you ever see it yourself?
Once, I saw it.

Can you describe it? But the voice disappears
In a rising roar like a jet engine,
A tearing, a stitch of silence. Something has been lost;
The voice resumes, quietly:
'The locks
Forced upward, a shift of air
Pulled over the head. The face bent
And the eyes winced, like craning
To look in the core of a furnace.
The man unravelled
Back to a snag, a dark thread'.

Then what happens?
The person disappears.
For a time he stays close by and speaks
In a child's voice. He is not seen, and
You must leave food out for him, and be careful
Where you throw water after you wash your feet.

And then he is gone?
                    He's gone, after a while.

You find this more strange than the yearly miracle
Of the loaf turning into a child?
Well, that's natural, she says,
I often baked the bread for that myself.

A Whole Life

Down here it's sheltered, and the children play
Rolling down the grass bank
And always roll crooked; we look up;
The temple cranes out over the hill,
Seeming to fall as the wind flourishes, through
Arches opening on blanks, gallops up tumbles
Of crooked stairs, around pillars weathered,
Sucked by every breath that's blown here since the Fall.

Never equipped with a graveyard or a kitchen midden,
There's nothing to dig, the foundations
Are sand, the level flags are too smooth
To show a date; it faces every way.

– Along the skyline pass two black monks
Bearing a weighty book with an iron clasp.
They march between the arches and can still be seen.

Thus, after the lessons, the warnings
From the lady with the French pleat and the colonel's cap
– *Remember, you will have only one chance* –
The skills work to perfection, the parachute spreads,
The wind is a slide conveying the graceful soldier
To a landing on soft, crusted snow.

Those People

When the four women tramp in sight
Dragging their children round the corner,
All the dolls in the shop windows look askance.
The shopkeepers know these people,
They are not going to leave,
They will remain visible,
Still there at three in the afternoon
When the shops are closed and the bars
Shutter their darkness, they will be
Out on the cobbles, beside the abandoned
Slimy fountain, hardly moving at all
But showing no definite signs of sleep.
At night their campfire will glow
– They will be cooking that stew,
Lifting the lid to stir it, and
The smell will blow all over
As it reeks now from their skirts.

The man at the cash-register
Beside the looped bead curtain says
I think myself it's the goat's milk.

The Promise

In retrospect, it is all edge;
The rivers crossed were all one river, at the edge
Of a wide roughened patch, one like
The mark of a blow, a mark for life;
The road linked the twin towns, falling
In loops, like a shadow in water.

There, like a beckoning arm, a tree
Ventured a rounded branch between
Streetpacked façades; the air expanded,
Eyes shot wider, skin responded,
Fingers shuffled, hidden
Pianissimo, stroking the minted
Edge. So a grave-thief
Breathes deep and bristles, if
A bare coin gleams
Between pelvic rags, a profile
Warm from the pocket of Constantine.

In retrospect, it was all
A prelude to the embarkation.
I watch the bones, and they begin to shine,

Where, like a welded scar, we show
Where we have split and healed askew –

You rock inside your skin
Your bones rock in your flesh
The full bottles in the duty-free shop
Rattle like bells on the soft waves.

Nothing is going to happen until we land.

PART TWO

The Rose-Geranium

The Last Glimpse of Erin

The coastline, a swimmer's polished shoulder heaving
On the edge of sky. Our eyes make it grow:
The last glimpse, low and smooth in the sea.

We face the air, all surfaces become
Sheer, one long line is growing
Like a spider's navel cord: the distance

From your low shoulder lost in the quilt,
An arm thrown forward — a swimmer — your head
Buried in a pillow like a wave.

The white light skirting the cloud pierces
Glass riddled with small scratches and creates
The depths and cadences of a spider's web.

A man is holding his baby and laughing,
He strokes her cheek with a brownstained finger
While his wife sews a wristbutton on his other hand.

The island trimmed with waves is lost in the sea,
The swimmer lost in his dream.

'He Hangs in Shades the Orange Bright'

So quiet the girl in the room
he says
'It is a precarious bowl
Of piled white eggs on a high shelf'

Against the dark wardrobe the gleam
Of skin and the damp hair inclining
Over her leaning shoulder fades
Into dark. She leans on a hand
Clutching the bedrail, her breasts pale
Askew as she stands looking left
Past the window towards the bright glass.
But from the window it is clear
That the dark glass reflects nothing;
Brilliance of the water-bottle
Spots the ceiling

The man in the courtyard waters the roots of the trees
And birds in their cages high on the red wall sing.

She moves her head and sees
The window tall on hinges
Each oblong tightly veiled. One side admits
Air through a grey slatted shutter, and light
Floats to the ceiling's
Profound white lake.

Still the sound of water and the stripe
Of blue sky and red wall,
Dark green leaves and fruit, one ripe orange
she says
'The sheet lightning over the mountains
As I drove over the quiet plain
Past the dark orange-groves'.

46

March 18th 1977

Waking with a sore head
A freshly bruised shin,
Forgetting the collision:
Eyes open and see
With relief, my coat on a hanger.
The early light that slants
Warm from the curtain lights up
The skin of your face,
Glittering all over like a lake in a sharp breeze —
The eyelids, those fine
Horizontal folds: like cliffs by a lake
Layered and loaded with flowers.

When my skin was as smooth as
A jamjar of water
I looked for time in my father's eyes:
Brown and green circling,
A bead of yellow under the corner
When no part of my body
Was more private than a fish
Going round and round in a jamjar of water.

The Rose-Geranium

1. *Like One Borne Away in a Dance and Veiled*

She learned again so soon
How the body is subdued
To all the laws that rule
The acorn's fall and the erosion of tall cliffs.

Like one borne away in a dance and veiled
She dreamed of a high house with shining floors
Where they squatted over stoves
And well-shod women held breath in the lift
If ever they went out or in.

They chewed into the side of the tower,
A fungus. From the night-time street
The rooms they had invaded showed —
Their half-light, their droning seeped.

And the day the building fell into the street
And blood fell and bodies folded and spun
The prisoner had company:

X-ray bones of snow,
Rivers grinding south,
Planes of ice bleeding at the edges downstream.

2. *She Opened the Egg*

When she opened the egg the wise woman had given her,
she found inside some of her own hair and a tooth, still
bloody, from her own mouth.

One summer after another
The shore advanced and receded
As the boat shoved past the islands.

Dark bushy hills revolved in the path;
                            and in each
Of the solid still rooms above bars,
                        the first sight
Caught at an angle, the glass questioning your face.

3. *Willaupuis*

'*A l'usage de M. et Mme van Gramberen*'
— the convent phrase (nothing is to be mine,
Everything ours) marks the small round enclosure,
Its table and bench. Distinguished
From the other old people, from the nuns' gravel
They sat in the windmill's afternoon shadow, half
Hidden by a moving carthorse's huge blond rump
And quarrelled over their sins for Saturday:
Examination of Conscience before Confession

Prepared and calm in case one thought
Struck them both, an attentive pose
Eluding me now, at ten in the morning, alone
With a clean college pantry: piled rings
Of glass rising, smooth as a weir.

The moment sways
Tall and soft as a poplar
Pointing into a lifetime of sky.

4.   *The Rose-Geranium*

The precious dry rose-geranium smell
Comes down with spirals of sunlit dust
From the high sill: nodding stems
Travelling out from the root
Embrace a fistful of dusk among the leaves.

The man sitting below, his head
Veiled in smoke, the face a cliff in shadow,
Waits: the sun in Scorpio climbs in
Dodging the fragrant leaves; and as subtly
As the eyes of two musicians touching
Light strokes his hair in place.

In spite of your long horizontal twilights
There is an instant when the sun meets the sea
Dividing light from dark
An hour when the shadow passes the mark on the wall
And the cloud of the rose-geranium dulls your hair.

5.   *The Pebble Skips*

Grace, the instant overloaded, the spine
Righting itself, treading water. A boy
Makes tea, leaning over the sink, his weight
Landed on one foot, riding —
That seahorse backbone, ruffled at the hip,
The breeze lifting, filling cloth . . .

Sloping westward, the roads
Of the body, drumlin shoulder,
Away from sight the legs angled
Like dry wood scaffolding
Overgrown and left behind.
I lie down
And start work with the ivy.

6. *Circus*

As if suddenly reincarnated
One lunch-hour as Saint
Sebastian, pierced and visible,
The weathercock loses his freedom to turn,
Crowds advance on him like the four winds.

And in the street, under
Transparent branches of trees
Single, fixed, waving softly,
Human figures wave their transparent hands.

Down to the roots not a pocket, a closet
Not a ledge of them hidden.
As they pass the fairground they revolve
And the roundabouts waver, lifting and falling.

In a line from the crossroads, beyond
The fountain and the gentlemen's lavatory,
The road at infinity appears to curve a little
As a branch in summer weighed down by the young fruit.

Although raised up, steady, he can't be sure.
The scene pierces him with claws like a lobster's,
And somewhere an eye sees him as a whirlpool of glass.

7. *Waters Between*

Gazing in the cold at the bright scene
I reach to stroke the pane revealing the garden;
And it melts at my touch into a wall
Where a thousand silver drops are turning, turning away.

8. *Waking*

In my dream I feel the shock of waking:
By the pillow, shadows of high branches,
Black rind and pale flower
Are signals from a garden drowned behind glass.
But between them, slipped alongside
Suburban Ranelagh, a narrow slice of land
Bears a fragile deck-cargo,
A small Protestant graveyard.

Lawn stumbles downhill over tombstones
(Roots of yew heave at the gravel path)
From the door of a low plain church;
And a black noticeboard, roofed for the rain,
Lettered in gold, stands sharply out
Against my decaying brick wall
More beautiful than the peartree's
Crowded black branches.

9. *Overmantel*

So rarely we lie
As then, in darkness
A vertical gleam relieved
Where the brilliance from outside
Struck the glass over the hearth

(Breast high, if one stood,
Night lapped the bookshelves
And a dying light floated
Above us, never reaching
Us, our arrested embrace)

I think at once of
That amphibious
Twilight, now that the year is
Revisiting the spring shrine.
At my window the sharp, grey

Rectangles of stone
Range, parade in squares.
February light
Spreading across the walls over my head
Washes my room with shadows, cold until morning.

10. *Skeleton Walk*

The bones wake up, reach
Like tendrils for support
They feel the air in their cavities
Thunder of racehorses comes to them in the earth.

And, lightly rising, they climb aloft on her shoulders.
At once her own bones are reminded — it is the same,
The pressure — the rim of the clavicle biting
As the long humerus idly swings by her side.

Empty as a diagram
The laughable straight lines
Even now hold secrets
Of pleasure and fatigue. She sleeps,
Her head in the dish of a pelvis:
She knows how they stir beneath her.

11. *Talking to the Skin*

Screening the piled
Loose knitting, slopes
Gorges, fences,
What leagues apart,
The eye pierces
A grid, selects:

Skin, a sardine fisher's
Net shaken to dry
In a breeze, waves gleaming back.

With a twitch tides change,
The dark flag bangs against a sunset wind.
Another window spreads:

Talking to the light that scatters on the skin,
The sun drags its web on over the ocean face
Like a memory giving back nothing but knots of brightness.
The flaw muscling with light
Creases, darkens, bubbles in tears, arrives.

12. *War's Annals Fading*

Linked by precious chains
The feathered shapes moved with her as she moved,
Still descending lava stairs
Between scrub and a scatter
Of pines waving on the slope.
The command was, not to look
Down, but she did and saw the shore:

An oval sea, with the gleam
Of an iron lid raised an instant,
The rough pebbles where no boat rested
Or wave stirred among the weed.

And beyond the inlet, beyond the stiff black trees
That circle the burnt-out island,
Still flying, nesting, the slim grey birds
Without a cry, those birds of whom
No history of shapes transformed
Or grief outlived is ever told.
They flourish there, by the subterranean sea.

13. *Feeding the Cats*

Because this is the age of his life
In retrospect he will name theirs
He calls now at noon to feed their cats;
And stretched on a chaise longue in the clean house
He bites one of the yellow sweet apples
Wrinkling in the dish, while the female
Noses his feet. The black cat watches him
From the padded rail at his elbow:
A short demanding stare;
                       he recalls
A hand that shut off day,
An eye so close to what it sought, half-blinded,
A collage of hair and upholstery.

Beyond the half-drawn curtain, past the trailing boughs
Of their proper domain,
A goldfinch lights up
Childhood's cramped retreats,
Covenants made in
The scarce blood of berries
That dry on the twig.

The cats his shortlived witnesses.

14. *Amelia*

Remembering her half-sister Amelia, that girl
Whose hips askew made every step seem upstairs,
The woman at the airport tells me that from her
One spring she bought the first small car.

After that it was trains and taxis for Amelia
For years and years, while the younger lay
In the car in a leafy mews in Dublin
Making love to a bald actor
Her elbow tightening
Linked through the steering-wheel.

She tells me, this hot noisy afternoon,
That Amelia now drives a car like a cabin-cruiser
In Halifax, Nova Scotia, where her husband
Fishes for lobster in short ice-free summers.